She Prays

60-Day Prayer-Guided Journal For Women

This Journal Belongs To:

_____

SHE PRAYS. Copyright © 2020. Clerol Austrie. All Rights Reserved.

Printed in the United States of America.

No portion of this book may be reproduced, stored in a retrieval system, or transmitted in any form or by any means, except for brief quotations in printed reviews, without the prior written permission of DayeLight Publishers or Clerol Austrie.

ISBN: 978-1-949343-84-7

Biography

Clerol Austrie is a spiritual leader, a Christian influencer, a faith strategist, a medical student, and a successful business owner. She was born and raised on the small island of Dominica. Her ability to lead, serve, and be effective in ministry was recognized at a very young age. The exposure to the Christian lifestyle through the life of her late grandmother and mother, encouraged her to get to know God for herself and recognize her place in the kingdom of God. Her upbringing built the foundation that initiated a connection between her and God that would lead her to later becoming a minister of the gospel and a pastor at her local church. However, Clerol did not yield to her calling without a fight.

Clerol went through her Jonah experience, where she wrestled with God and ran from her purpose. She went through many difficulties that she knew was due to her non-compliance with God. This initiated the beginning of her radical obedience and birthing of God's ministry. Pastor Austrie, now leads both an online and local ministry encouraging Christians to yield to God's plan and purpose for their lives. She encouraged others to live the life that God wants them to live by building a solid relationship with God and focusing on His instructions to them. Her ministry "Just Be You Movement" focuses on not imitating other people's definition of Christianity and not leaning on the world's definition of who they should be. Rather, to refer to their Creator and Source, who is God the Father, to understand His plan and to execute it even though it goes against the norms. She strongly believes that Jesus came so that we could learn how to live out our *Jeremiah 29:11* lives in abundance. She is appealing to you to "just be you" from God's point of view through fervent prayer and building your faith steadily in Jesus Christ.

How To Use This Journal

"She Prays" was written to help you to be consistent in prayer and meditating on the word of God. You will discover your prayer distractors and hindrances, so you can map out a strategy to overcome them and grow in God. You will find inside:

Tips on how to pray and how to create your own prayers.

This tool helps to avoid common issues that may have discouraged you from praying in the past, such as being lost for words or being too busy to pray.

Spiritual Goals

You will start each week by listing your spiritual goals for that specific week. This will help you to focus on identifying areas that need work and record it for accountability. Setting Spiritual goals to be achieved over one week makes your growth in God feel more attainable.

Weekly prayer planners

Plan your prayer sessions so you will not fail to pray; intentionally making a note of your prayer time and putting measures in place to keep you following your prayer plan.

Prayer wall

Making a note of what you want to pray about and who you would like to pray for is an effective strategy to ensure that your time with God is productive

Weekly Devotionals

It helps you to be consistent with your bible reading and to assist in targeting specific areas in your spiritual lives.

Daily thoughts

These thoughts are prompt ways to keep you seeking God and also promotes daily reflection, which can be used as talking points when in prayer.

Self-Reflection

The progress page allows for self-reflection where you may record your wins, growth, and areas that need additional focus.

Tips On Praying Effectively

In Matthew 6, Jesus gave us instructions on how to pray:

Tip 1:

Be aware of your heart and its intentions. It is important that we search ourselves in preparing for prayer. We always want to be aware of any ill-intent or self-righteousness. We must approach God humbly, willingly, and with every intention for Him alone to be glorified.

"And when you pray, do not be like the hypocrites, for they love to pray standing in the synagogues and on the street corners to be seen by others. Truly I tell you, they have received their reward in full." (Matthew 6:5 – NIV).

We should not pray to be seen or recognized by anyone. Praying in public is not the problem, but seeking recognition from the public is the problem. God is big on "the intent." God will allow the reward for your attention-seeking prayer only to be just that: ATTENTION, not from Him but the attention of the twos and threes that you have called to gather in YOUR name.

Tip 2:

Give God one on one time with you.

"But when you pray, go into your room, close the door and pray to your Father, who is unseen. Then your Father, who sees what is done in secret, will reward you." (Matthew 6:6 – NIV).

The most intimate prayers are the ones that are prayed in private with God. There is a certain level of intimacy that is achieved when you dedicate that un-corrupted and uninterrupted fellowship with God.

Create a prayer closet, prayer space, or prayer wall in your home. This strategy helps you to stay on top of your prayer life intentionally and minimize outside influences and distractions. Quiet time with God encourages you to present and expose yourself and your heart to God. It is also important to get the support of the ones you live with. Let it be clear that your prayer time is your time. Make necessary arrangements beforehand to avoid any interruptions. The enemy wants to distract your prayer flow, so ensure to leave nothing at his disposal to accomplish that. Although there are times that it will seem inevitable, always be persistent and consistent with your "DO NOT DISTURB" implementation. As promised, God will reward your efforts to seek Him intimately.

Tip 3:

Allow yourself to be transparent before God.

God wants all of you. He wants you to approach Him with the willingness to expose your good and your bad, your pains, and your joys. Drop the façade and forget about trying to sound intelligent, righteous, or spiritual. God wants the naked you and your naked truth. If you are hurt, in pain, or even bearing un-forgiveness, let Him know. Your confession is not to inform God, as He is omniscient, but it is to reveal to yourself how much you need God.

"And when you pray, do not keep on babbling like pagans, for they think they will be heard because of their many words. Do not be like them, for your Father knows what you need before you ask him." (Matthew 6:7-8 – NIV).

Additionally, pre-written prayers are absolutely useful. They give you an idea of different styles of prayers. God, however, wants us to pray meaningful prayers that reflects us and our needs, and not just mere recitals. Many don't pray because they feel like their words are redundant. If you feel that way, this Journal will definitely guide and help you work on that.

Prayer Structure

Having a structure in mind when praying allows the smooth flow of your words to God. This eliminates the awkward pausing, the stuttering, and incidental repetitions that may occur when we pray. Jesus saw it fit to give us a template to help us pray more effectively. Whether you are a newbie to the faith or a seasoned Christian, the structure of the Lord's prayer is an undeniably useful tool. So let's dive in!

"This, then, is how you should pray..." (Matthew 6:9 – NIV).

1) **Adoration:** "Our Father in heaven, hallowed be your name" (Matthew 6:9- NIV)

You must address whom you are praying to. We are to pray to the Father. You may address God as Lord, Heavenly Father, Almighty Father, Jehovah, just to name a few and open the conversation with adoration. Thank God for who He is (worship), and later, you may call Him out on what He has done for you (praise).

Personally, I dedicate extra time to this step when I pray. This very important introduction helps to open the door that leads to an atmospheric shift enabled by the Holy Spirit. This aligns your focus towards the things of God and gets you ready for a fervent and powerful prayer session. In this manner, you invite and welcome the Holy Spirit to move in all of His power and take over.

2) **Surrender to His Will:** *"Your kingdom come, your will be done, on earth as it is in heaven." (Matthew 6:10 – NIV)*. Rendering your desires and your will over to God in exchange for His, helps you to stay in line with God's plan.

You may have many plans for your life, but ultimately, life will show you that only God's plans will prevail. There is no need to fight God, rush God, or bargain with Him to get your way. He knows the plans He has for you, and your desire should be to yield to that by all means necessary.

Do two walk together unless they have agreed to do so? (Amos 3:3 – NIV).

3) **Prayer Requests:** *"Give us today our daily bread"*– *(Matthew 6:11 – NIV)*. The Lord promised to supply all our needs and encourages us to ask, and we will receive, not according to the need that we have, but according to the Lord's riches. He promises to bless us and give us our heart's desires. So go

boldly before the Lord. It is also important that we do not focus only on our physical needs but on our mental, emotional, and spiritual needs as well.

4) **Forgiveness:** *"And forgive us our debts, as we also have forgiven our debtors." (Matthew 6:12 -NIV).*

Bring your wrongdoings to God and ask for forgiveness. We tear ourselves away from God when we remain in our sin. Sin separates us from Him (See Isaiah 59:2). Also, God will not forgive us if we do not free ourselves from those who have sinned against us (See Matthew 6:15).

5) **Protection, deliverance from the enemy and our flesh**: *"And lead us not into temptation, but deliver us from the evil one." (Matthew 6:13 - NIV).* The bible gives you many assurances and guidelines on how to deal and identify the evil one. God will not let us be tempted beyond what you can bear. But when you are tempted, He will also provide a way out so that you can endure it (See 1 Corinthians 10:13). God provides a way of escape, so we do not fall victim, but we are to lean on Him to take the way of escape successfully.

Note that we wrestle not against flesh and blood, so it is important to note that your enemy is not your co-worker who is trying to get you fired, nor your neighbor who insists on blasting music at crazy hours of the night. You must know your enemy in order to fight appropriately and win!

Prayer Styling

Build Your Prayers

Ways to address God:

Yahweh - The Lord

Abba - Father: (See Galatians 4:6).

El Elyon - God Most High: (See Psalm 7:17).

El Roi - The God who sees: (See Genesis 16:13).

El Shaddai - God Almighty: (See Psalm 91:1).

Yahweh/Jehovah Jireh - The Lord will provide: (See Genesis 22:14).

Yahweh / Jehovah Nissi - The Lord is my banner: (See Exodus 17:15).

Jehovah Rapha – The God who heals: (See Exodus 15:26).

Yahweh/Jehovah Shalom: Lord of Peace: (See Judges 6:24).

Recognition of who God is: Who is God to you?

_____

_____

_____

Recognition of what God has done: How have you seen God work around you?

_____

_____

_____

Surrender: How do your desires or activities stand in the way of you getting closer to God?

_____

_____

_____

Forgiving others: Who do you need to forgive, and why?

_____

_____

_____

Request for forgiveness: In what ways have you hurt God (could be in actions, words, or meditation)

_____

_____

_____

Prayer Requests: Write down the names of the people you want to cover in prayer.

_____

_____

_____

Protection, deliverance from the enemy, and our flesh: What are the ways do you often fall victim to the enemy's temptation, lies, or surrender to the ungodly demands of your flesh (e.g., ego, pride, envy, greed, etc.)?

_____

_____

_____

_____

_____

She Prays...

...and that makes her powerful.

Spiritual Goals for this Week

Prayer Plan For This Week

MONDAY

MY PRAYER TIME:

OBSTACLES THAT MAY PREVENT ME FROM PRAYING THAT DAY.

HOW WILL I AVOID OR OVERCOME?

TUESDAY

MY PRAYER TIME:

OBSTACLES THAT MAY PREVENT ME FROM PRAYING THAT DAY.

HOW WILL I AVOID OR OVERCOME?

WEDNESDAY

MY PRAYER TIME:

OBSTACLES THAT MAY PREVENT ME FROM PRAYING THAT DAY.

HOW WILL I AVOID OR OVERCOME?

Prayer Plan For This Week

THURSDAY

MY PRAYER TIME:

OBSTACLES THAT MAY PREVENT ME FROM PRAYING THAT DAY.

HOW WILL I AVOID OR OVERCOME?

FRIDAY

MY PRAYER TIME:

OBSTACLES THAT MAY PREVENT ME FROM PRAYING THAT DAY.

HOW WILL I AVOID OR OVERCOME?

SATURDAY

MY PRAYER TIME:

OBSTACLES THAT MAY PREVENT ME FROM PRAYING THAT DAY.

HOW WILL I AVOID OR OVERCOME?

Prayer Plan For This Week

NOTES

SUNDAY

MY PRAYER TIME:

OBSTACLES THAT MAY PREVENT ME FROM PRAYING THAT DAY.

HOW WILL I AVOID OR OVERCOME?

Prayer Wall

Faith Building

Week 1 Devotional

"And without faith, it is impossible to please God, because anyone who comes to Him must believe that He exists and that He rewards those who earnestly seek Him." (Hebrews 11:6 – NIV).

There are many levels of faith. In John 3:16, *it says that God loved the world so much that He gave His only Son so that anyone who believes in Him will have everlasting life.* This particular passage indicates that your faith in Jesus Christ will secure your spot in heaven. In Hebrew 11: 6, faith is being mentioned again, but this time, faith is tied to pleasing God. It mentions that whoever approaches Him must first believe He is God, and secondly, must come expecting a reward as He is a rewarder of those who seek Him. Coming to God with expectancy is pleasing to Him, and He will not allow you to leave empty-handed.

God wants us to come to Him, fully convinced that He is able and willing to do anything we ask or think. Your faith will make you whole, pleasing, and acceptable to God. As you might have gathered, there is power in your faith. There is the power to please and the power to receive. Believing God for what you want automatically puts you at an advantage. However, that power will pique the interest of the enemy, so be on the alert. The enemy has crafted ways to influence you to stop believing and to doubt that God will come through for you. He needs you to doubt because doubt nullifies your prayer (See James 1:6-8).

How to combat doubt: Ask of God and believe, but when it seems like you are not getting what you've prayed for, begin looking out for a better answer to your prayer.

Here is the reason: The promise that all things will work together for the good of them that love the Lord (See Romans 8:28) confirms that whatever God is going to do about your situation will work out in your best interest. Never doubt that God will answer your prayer, simply expect an answer that will work out even better for you than the one you requested and wait expecting it. Go about your day, expecting that surprising answer at any given moment.

Day 1: _____

Day Time Thoughts

Today's prayer:

_____

_____

_____

_____

Bible Verse(s) I will meditate on today:

_____

_____

_____

_____

Today, I will work on:

_____

_____

_____

_____

_____

Day 1: _____

Nighttime Thoughts

Today, God showed me:

_____

_____

_____

_____

What I did differently today that helped me feel closer to God:

_____

_____

_____

_____

I helped someone today by:

_____

_____

_____

_____

Day 2: _____

Day Time Thoughts

Today's prayer:

_____

_____

_____

_____

Bible Verse(s) I will meditate on today:

_____

_____

_____

_____

Today, I affirm:

_____

_____

_____

_____

_____

Day 2: _____

Nighttime Thoughts

Today, I stepped out in faith by:

_____

_____

_____

_____

And it made me feel:

_____

_____

_____

I spent time with God by:

_____

_____

_____

_____

Day 3: _____

Day Time Thoughts

Today's prayer:

_____
_____
_____
_____

Bible Verse(s) I will meditate on today:

_____
_____
_____

I'm trusting God to:

_____
_____
_____
_____

Day 3: _____

Nighttime Thoughts

Today, I obeyed God by:

_____

_____

_____

_____

Today, I started/stopped:

_____

_____

_____

_____

Today, I was honest with God about:

_____

_____

_____

_____

Day 4: _____

Day Time Thoughts

Today's prayer:

_____

_____

_____

_____

Bible Verse(s) I will meditate on today:

_____

_____

_____

_____

Today, I speak over:

_____

_____

_____

_____

Day 4: _____

Nighttime Thoughts

I would describe today as:

_____

_____

_____

_____

I'm making it easier for God to direct me by:

_____

_____

_____

_____

Today, I forgave/started working on forgiving:

_____

_____

_____

_____

_____

Day 5: _____

Day Time Thoughts

Today's prayer:

_____

_____

_____

_____

Bible Verse(s) I will meditate on today:

_____

_____

_____

_____

Today, I believe:

_____

_____

_____

_____

_____

_____

Day 5: _____

Nighttime Thoughts

Today, I learned:

_____

_____

_____

Based on today, I will start to work on:

_____

_____

_____

Today, I see growth:

_____

_____

_____

Day 6: _____

Day Time Thoughts

Today's prayer:

_____

_____

_____

_____

Bible Verse(s) I will meditate on today:

_____

_____

_____

Today, I declare:

_____

_____

_____

_____

_____

Day 6: _____

Nighttime Thoughts

I showed love today by:

_____
_____
_____
_____

Today, I followed God by:

_____
_____
_____
_____

Today, I became aware of:

_____
_____
_____
_____

Day 7: _____

Day Time Thoughts

Today's prayer:

_____

_____

_____

_____

Bible Verse(s) I will meditate on today:

_____

_____

_____

Today, I trust God for:

_____

_____

_____

_____

Day 7: _____

Nighttime Thoughts

Today, I resisted the enemy by:

_____

_____

_____

_____

I felt God's presence today when:

_____

_____

_____

_____

I want to begin:

_____

_____

_____

_____

Self-Reflection

Week 1 Spiritual Progress

She Prays...

...and waits on

The Lord.

Spiritual Goals for This Week

Prayer Plan For This Week

MONDAY

MY PRAYER TIME:

OBSTACLES THAT MAY PREVENT ME FROM PRAYING THAT DAY.

HOW WILL I AVOID OR OVERCOME?

TUESDAY

MY PRAYER TIME:

OBSTACLES THAT MAY PREVENT ME FROM PRAYING THAT DAY.

HOW WILL I AVOID OR OVERCOME?

WEDNESDAY

MY PRAYER TIME:

OBSTACLES THAT MAY PREVENT ME FROM PRAYING THAT DAY.

HOW WILL I AVOID OR OVERCOME?

Prayer Plan For This Week

THURSDAY

MY PRAYER TIME:

OBSTACLES THAT MAY PREVENT ME FROM PRAYING THAT DAY.

HOW WILL I AVOID OR OVERCOME?

FRIDAY

MY PRAYER TIME:

OBSTACLES THAT MAY PREVENT ME FROM PRAYING THAT DAY.

HOW WILL I AVOID OR OVERCOME?

SATURDAY

MY PRAYER TIME:

OBSTACLES THAT MAY PREVENT ME FROM PRAYING THAT DAY.

HOW WILL I AVOID OR OVERCOME?

Prayer Plan For This Week

NOTES

SUNDAY

MY PRAYER TIME:

OBSTACLES THAT MAY PREVENT ME FROM PRAYING THAT DAY.

HOW WILL I AVOID OR OVERCOME?

Prayer Wall

A Woman After God's Own Heart

Week 2 Devotional

"Would you let my father and mother come and stay with you until I know what God will do for me?" (1 Samuel 22:3b – NIV).

"Let me see what God will do for me," was David's reaction when he was marked to be murdered by King Saul. David did what he could to preserve his life by hiding, but he was still expecting while actively being hunted down, that God would do something about his situation. From David's point of view, it looked like the end was near. He was in full flight or fight mode, yet he waited on God. Based on David's reaction, one can identify why God considered him to be a man after His own heart. Not because he was sinless, perfect and without any tendency to make bad decisions but David's heart sought after God intentionally even when faced with death.

Are you a woman after God's own heart? Are you chasing after God's decisions about your life? Are you seeking God with every fiber of your being when eviction, sickness, betrayal, malice, or even death is chasing after you?

There is no difference between you and David, except for the obvious aspect of gender. You have slain giants just as he has. You have sung praises to the Lord and sought-after God just the same. You are seeking after God right now as you read this devotional. YOU ARE A WOMAN AFTER GOD'S OWN HEART.

Say it out loud: "I'm a woman after God's own heart"

Write it down: _____

Now, get ready to act like it and make it official. Every day, chase God, chase the thoughts of God, chase after the will of God by being at alert, and expecting God to come through for you.

Act like a woman after God's own heart by waiting to see what God will do for you concerning the situation you are facing.

Let God know that you are waiting to see what He will do for you and if someone asks about your situation, declare to them that you are waiting to see what God will do for you.

When the devil comes to inquire by initiating anxiety and panic, let the anxiety and panic know that you are waiting on God to see what He will do for you because He promised to provide all of your needs according to His riches in glory.

Do not be tricked into blindly accepting any and every possible solution. Wait until you see God in it because God is the Gentleman, who opens doors for you!

Day 1: _____

Day Time Thoughts

Today's prayer:

_____
_____
_____
_____

Bible Verse(s) I will meditate on today:

_____
_____
_____

Today, I will work on:

_____
_____
_____
_____
_____

Day 1: _____

Nighttime Thoughts

Today, God showed me:

_____

_____

_____

_____

What I did differently today that helped me feel closer to God:

_____

_____

_____

_____

I helped someone today by:

_____

_____

_____

_____

Day 2: _____

Day Time Thoughts

Today's prayer:

_____
_____
_____
_____

Bible Verse(s) I will meditate on today:

_____
_____
_____
_____

Today, I affirm:

_____
_____
_____
_____
_____

Day 2: _____

Nighttime Thoughts

Today, I stepped out in faith by:

_____
_____
_____
_____

And it made me feel:

_____
_____
_____
_____

I spent time with God by:

_____
_____
_____
_____

Day 3: _____

Day Time Thoughts

Today's prayer:

_____
_____
_____
_____

Bible Verse(s) I will meditate on today:

_____
_____
_____
_____

I'm trusting God to:

_____
_____
_____
_____
_____

Day 3: _____

Nighttime Thoughts

Today, I obeyed God by:

_____

_____

_____

Today, I started/stopped:

_____

_____

_____

Today, I was honest with God about:

_____

_____

_____

_____

Day 4: _____

Day Time Thoughts

Today's prayer:

_____
_____
_____
_____

Bible Verse(s) I will meditate on today:

_____
_____
_____
_____

Today, I speak over:

_____
_____
_____
_____

Day 4: _____

Nighttime Thoughts

I would describe today as:

_____

_____

_____

_____

I'm making it easier for God to direct me by:

_____

_____

_____

_____

Today, I forgave/started working on forgiving:

_____

_____

_____

_____

Day 5: _____

Day Time Thoughts

Today's prayer:

_____
_____
_____
_____

Bible Verse(s) I will meditate on today:

_____
_____
_____
_____

Today, I believe:

_____
_____
_____
_____

Day 5: _____

Nighttime Thoughts

Today, I learned:

_____
_____
_____
_____

Based on today, I will start to work on:

_____
_____
_____
_____

Today, I see growth:

_____
_____
_____
_____

Day 6: _____

Day Time Thoughts

Today's prayer:

_____
_____
_____
_____

Bible Verse(s) I will meditate on today:

_____
_____
_____

Today, I declare:

_____
_____
_____
_____

Day 6: _____

Nighttime Thoughts

I showed love today by:

_____

_____

_____

_____

Today, I followed God by:

_____

_____

_____

_____

Today, I became aware of:

_____

_____

_____

_____

Day 7: _____

Day Time Thoughts

Today's prayer:

_____
_____
_____
_____

Bible Verse(s) I will meditate on today:

_____
_____
_____
_____

Today, I trust God for:

_____
_____
_____
_____
_____

Day 7: _____

Nighttime Thoughts

Today, I resisted the enemy by:

_____
_____
_____
_____

I felt God's presence today when:

_____
_____
_____
_____

I want to begin:

_____
_____
_____
_____

Self-Reflection

Week 2 Spiritual Progress

_____

_____

_____

_____

_____

_____

_____

_____

_____

_____

_____

_____

She Prays...

...and her

strength is

renewed.

Spiritual Goals for This Week

Prayer Plan For This Week

WEDNESDAY

MY PRAYER TIME:

OBSTACLES THAT MAY PREVENT ME FROM PRAYING THAT DAY.

HOW WILL I AVOID OR OVERCOME?

TUESDAY

MY PRAYER TIME:

OBSTACLES THAT MAY PREVENT ME FROM PRAYING THAT DAY.

HOW WILL I AVOID OR OVERCOME?

MONDAY

MY PRAYER TIME:

OBSTACLES THAT MAY PREVENT ME FROM PRAYING THAT DAY.

HOW WILL I AVOID OR OVERCOME?

Prayer Plan For This Week

THURSDAY

MY PRAYER TIME:

OBSTACLES THAT MAY PREVENT ME FROM PRAYING THAT DAY.

HOW WILL I AVOID OR OVERCOME?

FRIDAY

MY PRAYER TIME:

OBSTACLES THAT MAY PREVENT ME FROM PRAYING THAT DAY.

HOW WILL I AVOID OR OVERCOME?

SATURDAY

MY PRAYER TIME:

OBSTACLES THAT MAY PREVENT ME FROM PRAYING THAT DAY.

HOW WILL I AVOID OR OVERCOME?

Prayer Plan For This Week

NOTES

SUNDAY

MY PRAYER TIME:

OBSTACLES THAT MAY PREVENT ME FROM PRAYING THAT DAY.

HOW WILL I AVOID OR OVERCOME?

Prayer Wall

Faith Can't Grow In Comfort

Week 3 Devotional

"I consider that our present sufferings are not worth comparing with the glory that will be revealed in us." (Romans 8:18 – NIV).

Life gets really tough, and although God has offered Himself as a burden reliever for us (See 1Peter 5:7), we still feel the pressure and the strain from changes that occur in our lives. At times, it feels like everything that could go wrong does, all at the same time. However, as believers, our reaction to our disappointments and tough times reveals to us just how much we need God to keep working on us.

How do you react when things seem to have taken a turn for the worst?

We are encouraged to avoid interpreting our tough situations according to what we can understand, and instead, bring them to God to get His view of it. (See Proverbs 3:5-6). God is saying to you that what it looks like right now is not what it really is nor how it will continue to be. We are commanded to be anxious for and about nothing. Sometimes what we see, with our human eyes and what we analyze with our human mind, drives us to a place of panic. God has asked us to approach life by faith and not by sight (See 2 Corinthians 5:7). We must understand that God has plans for us, plans to prosper us (although prosperity may not seem to be anywhere near), and not harm us (although we feel like this storm is going to crush us). We need to speak God's truth to ourselves until we see it come to pass.

Do not allow what seems to be the big picture, to drown out the true picture. A SHIFT IS COMING!

If everything stays the same and remains comfortable, then there is no room for change. Faith cannot grow in comfort. God must create room for movement, room for improvement, and room for progress. There is no room for greatness in your comfort zone. It is natural for us to fear change and seek to find comfort in what we are used to. However, your inability to predict the outcome should not scare you. It should relieve you to know that what is out of your control, is still in God's sight and under His control.

In the bible, we see so many women who, although their names were not always mentioned, the stories of their faith in God lived on. Their decision to trust God even when things looked bad, has birthed so many ministries and movements today.

Let's take a look at their stories:

The Shunammite Woman- 2 Kings 4:8-37

A woman that was blessed with a child due to her willingness to serve the man of God, Elisha. She had totally given up on having a child before that encounter. Unfortunately, the child fell ill and died. However, instead of giving up and burying the child, she sought God through His servant, Elisha, and the child was brought back to life.

The Woman With The Issue Of Blood -Mark 5:25-32

After 12 years of battling an illness that was draining her and her pockets, she never gave up on finding a cure. Though she was weak and considered unclean due to her consistent bleeding, her faith was in top shape. Even in her physical weakness, she pushed through a crowd, motivated by the belief that if she could only touch the cloth of Jesus, she would be healed. Her faith brought her years of suffering to an end.

Story of Esther Saving Her People- Esther 4 and 5

Esther stepped out of what she was allowed to do and be as a woman in her time. She put herself in harm's way to seek the mercy of the king on behalf of her people. However this was not before she prayed and fasted to allow God to guide her and go before her. In the end, victory was hers.

If your life had to be placed in the bible, what would your story of faith be?

Write your story:

_____

_____

_____

_____

_____

_____

_____

_____

Day 1: _____

Day Time Thoughts

Today's prayer:

_____

_____

_____

_____

Bible Verse(s) I will meditate on today:

_____

_____

_____

_____

Today, I will work on:

_____

_____

_____

_____

Day 1: _____

Nighttime Thoughts

Today God showed me:

_____
_____
_____
_____

What I did differently today that helped me feel closer to God:

_____
_____
_____
_____

I helped someone today by:

_____
_____
_____
_____

Day 2: _____

Day Time Thoughts

Today's prayer:

_____

_____

_____

_____

Bible Verse(s) I will meditate on today:

_____

_____

_____

_____

Today, I affirm:

_____

_____

_____

_____

Day 2: _____

Nighttime Thoughts

Today, I stepped out in faith by:

_____
_____
_____
_____

And it made me feel:

_____
_____
_____
_____

I spent time with God by:

_____
_____
_____
_____

Day 3: _____

Day Time Thoughts

Today's prayer:

_____
_____
_____
_____

Bible Verse(s) I will meditate on today:

_____
_____
_____
_____

I'm trusting God to:

_____
_____
_____
_____

Day 3: _____

Nighttime Thoughts

Today, I obeyed God by:

_____
_____
_____
_____

Today, I started/stopped:

_____
_____
_____
_____

Today, I was honest with God about:

_____
_____
_____
_____

Day 4: _____

Day Time Thoughts

Today's prayer:

_____
_____
_____
_____

Bible Verse(s) I will meditate on today:

_____
_____
_____
_____

Today, I speak over:

_____
_____
_____
_____
_____

Day 4: _____

Nighttime Thoughts

I would describe today as:

_____
_____
_____
_____

I'm making it easier for God to direct me by:

_____
_____
_____
_____

Today, I forgave/started working on forgiving:

_____
_____
_____
_____
_____

Day 5: _____

Day Time Thoughts

Today's prayer:

_____

_____

_____

_____

Bible Verse(s) I will meditate on today:

_____

_____

_____

_____

Today, I believe:

_____

_____

_____

_____

_____

Day 5: _____

Nighttime Thoughts

Today, I learned:

_____

_____

_____

_____

Based on today, I will start to work on:

_____

_____

_____

_____

Today, I see growth:

_____

_____

_____

_____

Day 6: _____

Day Time Thoughts

Today's prayer:

_____
_____
_____
_____

Bible Verse(s) I will meditate on today:

_____
_____
_____
_____

Today, I declare:

_____
_____
_____
_____

Day 6: _____

Nighttime Thoughts

I showed love today by:

_____
_____
_____
_____

Today, I followed God by:

_____
_____
_____
_____

Today, I became aware of:

_____
_____
_____
_____

Day 7: _____

Day Time Thoughts

Today's prayer:

_____
_____
_____
_____

Bible Verse(s) I will meditate on today:

_____
_____
_____
_____

Today, I trust God for:

_____
_____
_____
_____

Day 7: _____

Nighttime Thoughts

Today, I resisted the enemy by:

_____
_____
_____
_____

I felt God's presence today when:

_____
_____
_____
_____

I want to begin:

_____
_____
_____
_____

Self-Reflection

Week 3 Spiritual Progress

_____
_____
_____
_____
_____
_____
_____
_____
_____
_____
_____
_____
_____
_____
_____

She Prays...

...and everything

attached to her

wins!

Spiritual Goals for This Week

Prayer Plan For This Week

MONDAY

MY PRAYER TIME:

OBSTACLES THAT MAY PREVENT ME FROM PRAYING THAT DAY.

HOW WILL I AVOID OR OVERCOME?

TUESDAY

MY PRAYER TIME:

OBSTACLES THAT MAY PREVENT ME FROM PRAYING THAT DAY.

HOW WILL I AVOID OR OVERCOME?

WEDNESDAY

MY PRAYER TIME:

OBSTACLES THAT MAY PREVENT ME FROM PRAYING THAT DAY.

HOW WILL I AVOID OR OVERCOME?

Prayer Plan For This Week

SATURDAY

MY PRAYER TIME:

OBSTACLES THAT MAY PREVENT ME FROM PRAYING THAT DAY.

HOW WILL I AVOID OR OVERCOME?

FRIDAY

MY PRAYER TIME:

OBSTACLES THAT MAY PREVENT ME FROM PRAYING THAT DAY.

HOW WILL I AVOID OR OVERCOME?

THURSDAY

MY PRAYER TIME:

OBSTACLES THAT MAY PREVENT ME FROM PRAYING THAT DAY.

HOW WILL I AVOID OR OVERCOME?

Prayer Plan For This Week

NOTES

SUNDAY

MY PRAYER TIME:

OBSTACLES THAT MAY PREVENT ME FROM PRAYING THAT DAY.

HOW WILL I AVOID OR OVERCOME?

Prayer Wall

You Are Still Blessed

Week 4 Devotional

"Blessed are the poor in spirit, for theirs is the kingdom of heaven. Blessed are those who mourn, for they will be comforted. Blessed are the meek, for they will inherit the earth. Blessed are those who hunger and thirst for righteousness, for they will be filled. Blessed are the merciful, for they will be shown mercy. Blessed are the pure in heart, for they will see God. Blessed are the peacemakers, for they will be called children of God. Blessed are those who are persecuted because of righteousness, for theirs is the kingdom of heaven. Blessed are you when people insult you, persecute you and falsely say all kinds of evil against you because of me." (Matthew 5:3-11 – NIV).

We often consider ourselves and others to be blessed based on how healthy our bank accounts look and on account of what we own. We count our blessings based on what makes us feel and look good. The world's idea of being blessed is based on property, which is entirely irrelevant to our eternity.

These material things do not make it beyond this life, and they won't help us to get to heaven.

I cannot find anywhere in the bible where we are told, "Blessed are those who own cars, have houses or healthy bank accounts." Being blessed is not about what you have, but WHO you have. It is easy to get distracted by everything that is going wrong in your life, but God sees the state of your life and the trust you continue to have in Him as a perfect opportunity to show you what your faith can do. What appears to you as a dead end, God allowed for a new beginning. What you see as a failure, God allowed as a step to success. God has every plan to prosper you, but remember, He is more concerned with you spending eternity with Him. God wants you to succeed spiritually, to reach spiritual milestones and not only achieve materialistic goals.

Do not get carried away with the world's definition of "being blessed." Do not conform to their requirements but allow yourself to be transformed by what God considers worthy of special treatment. The world will not reward you for doing what is right and pleasing to God. At times you will find that not even the church will reward you for your efforts, but your focus should not be on human applauds, acceptance or admiration. Yes, it does feel good to be recognized by people, but note that God is the rewarder of your faith, not humans.

Pay close attention to what moves, motivates, and influences you daily. Is it to have what others have? Is it so that you can flaunt all your possessions before the world? Would you care who you had to step on or push down to get it all?

Go into reflection at the end of every day to analyze your actions and reactions with God. Get to the root of it all and up-root any seeds planted that are not of God. Through prayer and intentional change in behavior, God will continue to perfect His will in your life. Every new day is another opportunity to do better.

You are still blessed and highly favored by the Lord, even when you have nothing materialistic to show for it. May your heart and your character show it all.

Day 1: _____

Day Time Thoughts

Today's prayer:

_____
_____
_____
_____

Bible Verse(s) I will meditate on today:

_____
_____
_____
_____

Today, I will work on:

_____
_____
_____
_____
_____

Day 1: _____

Nighttime Thoughts

Today God showed me:

_____

_____

_____

_____

What I did differently today that helped me feel closer to God:

_____

_____

_____

_____

I helped someone today by:

_____

_____

_____

_____

Day 2: _____

Day Time Thoughts

Today's prayer:

_____
_____
_____
_____

Bible Verse(s) I will meditate on today:

_____
_____
_____
_____

Today, I affirm:

_____
_____
_____
_____

Day 2: _____

Nighttime Thoughts

Today, I stepped out in faith by:

_____

_____

_____

_____

And it made me feel:

_____

_____

_____

_____

I spent time with God by:

_____

_____

_____

_____

Day 3: _____

Day Time Thoughts

Today's prayer:

_____
_____
_____

Bible Verse(s) I will meditate on today:

_____
_____
_____

I'm trusting God to:

_____
_____
_____
_____

Day 3: _____

Nighttime Thoughts

Today, I obeyed God by:

_____
_____
_____
_____

Today, I started/stopped:

_____
_____
_____
_____

Today, I was honest with God about:

_____
_____
_____
_____

Day 4: _____

Day Time Thoughts

Today's prayer:

_____
_____
_____
_____

Bible Verse(s) I will meditate on today:

_____
_____
_____
_____

Today, I speak over:

_____
_____
_____
_____
_____

Day 4: _____

Nighttime Thoughts

I would describe today as:

_____
_____
_____
_____

I'm making it easier for God to direct me by:

_____
_____
_____
_____

Today, I forgave/started working on forgiving:

_____
_____
_____
_____
_____

Day 5: _____

Day Time Thoughts

Today's prayer:

_____

_____

_____

_____

Bible Verse(s) I will meditate on today:

_____

_____

_____

_____

Today, I believe:

_____

_____

_____

_____

Day 5: _____

Nighttime Thoughts

Today, I learned:

_____
_____
_____
_____

Based on today, I will start to work on:

_____
_____
_____
_____

Today, I see growth:

_____
_____
_____
_____

Day 6: _____

Day Time Thoughts

Today's prayer:

_____
_____
_____
_____

Bible Verse(s) I will meditate on today:

_____
_____
_____
_____

Today, I declare:

_____
_____
_____
_____

Day 6: _____

Nighttime Thoughts

I showed love today by:

_____
_____
_____
_____

Today, I followed God by:

_____
_____
_____
_____

Today, I became aware of:

_____
_____
_____
_____

Day 7: _____

Day Time Thoughts

Today's prayer:

_____

_____

_____

_____

Bible Verse(s) I will meditate on today:

_____

_____

_____

_____

Today, I trust God for:

_____

_____

_____

_____

Day 7: _____

Nighttime Thoughts

Today, I resisted the enemy by:

_____
_____
_____
_____

I felt God's presence today when:

_____
_____
_____
_____

I want to begin:

_____
_____
_____
_____

Self-Reflection

Week 4 Spiritual Progress

_____
_____
_____
_____
_____
_____
_____
_____
_____
_____
_____
_____
_____
_____
_____
_____

She Prays...

...and victory

follows her.

Spiritual Goals for This Week

Prayer Plan For This Week

MONDAY

MY PRAYER TIME:

OBSTACLES THAT MAY PREVENT ME FROM PRAYING THAT DAY.

HOW WILL I AVOID OR OVERCOME?

TUESDAY

MY PRAYER TIME:

OBSTACLES THAT MAY PREVENT ME FROM PRAYING THAT DAY.

HOW WILL I AVOID OR OVERCOME?

WEDNESDAY

MY PRAYER TIME:

OBSTACLES THAT MAY PREVENT ME FROM PRAYING THAT DAY.

HOW WILL I AVOID OR OVERCOME?

Prayer Plan For This Week

THURSDAY

MY PRAYER TIME:

OBSTACLES THAT MAY PREVENT ME FROM PRAYING THAT DAY.

HOW WILL I AVOID OR OVERCOME?

FRIDAY

MY PRAYER TIME:

OBSTACLES THAT MAY PREVENT ME FROM PRAYING THAT DAY.

HOW WILL I AVOID OR OVERCOME?

SATURDAY

MY PRAYER TIME:

OBSTACLES THAT MAY PREVENT ME FROM PRAYING THAT DAY.

HOW WILL I AVOID OR OVERCOME?

Prayer Plan For This Week

NOTES

SUNDAY

MY PRAYER TIME:

OBSTACLES THAT MAY PREVENT ME FROM PRAYING THAT DAY.

HOW WILL I AVOID OR OVERCOME?

Prayer Wall

Own It!

Week 5 Devotional

"And he shall be like a tree planted by the rivers of water, that bringeth forth his fruit in his season; his leaf also shall not wither; and whatsoever he doeth shall prosper." (Psalms 1:3 – KJV).

Every one of us is in a different season in our lives. Some of us are in a dry season, where the results of our hard work are not yet seen. Some may be in a silent season, where we have not yet received the answers to our prayers. This may cause you to feel like God has forgotten or overlooked you. You may be wondering if He no longer deems you loyal, faithful or even holy enough to make things better in your life. The length of your season may be wearing you out!

Sis, your attitude towards God and your belief in His promises should never be controlled by or be dependent on what season you are in. It does not matter what your immediate situation is. God's promises to you have not changed, and His love for you will not dissipate. It is easy to be excited about

God's blessings when you can see them. But I encourage you to be just as excited about your blessing even when you have to "faith" them. When you see nothing, God's sweet words to you should be the evidence on which you build your faith.

Do not wait until you see God's promises physically come to pass for you to believe that you are blessed and highly favored and that your answer is on its way.

Do not wait for physical manifestations of your answered prayers before you make the intentional decision to rejoice in the Lord.

We are to rejoice in the Lord always, especially when our naked eyes see nothing to rejoice about. For the Word of God says, *"blessed are those who have not seen and yet have believed"* (John 20:29b - NIV).

It is the season to live intentionally and purposefully. You will no longer settle and make decisions with the mentality that you are not good enough, holy enough, blessed enough, or gifted enough. You may not be worthy of God's blessings, nor of His mercies and grace; none of us are. But if He sees it fit to give you His Word and promises to prosper you, even though He has seen the deepest parts of you, who are you then to walk around feeling defeated.

When the physical evidence of God's presence and His promises is not yet seen, that does not change a thing.

No matter what season you are in, THIS IS YOUR SEASON, so own it. Learn whatever it is you were placed there to learn.

This is the season to stop comparing your worth to others and own who God says that you are.

This is the season to start walking in power and OWN IT.

This is the season to walk into situations, filled with the promise and anticipation of God's miracles and OWN IT.

This is the season to take back what the devil stole and get your double portion

This is the season to stop giving the devil authority over your life that was redeemed by the blood of the Lamb.

According to God, through Him, you are more than a conqueror (See Romans 8:37). Today, refuse to listen to the lies that the enemy wants you to believe. Would you ever take directions from a blind man? Then, don't take advice about your life from a dead man (the devil), to whom salvation is not offered, and God's promise does not apply to.

Day 1: _____

Day Time Thoughts

Today's prayer:

_____

_____

_____

_____

Bible Verse(s) I will meditate on today:

_____

_____

_____

_____

Today, I will work on:

_____

_____

_____

_____

_____

Day 1: _____

Nighttime Thoughts

Today God showed me:

_____
_____
_____
_____

What I did differently today that helped me feel closer to God:

_____
_____
_____
_____

I helped someone today by:

_____
_____
_____
_____

Day 2: _____

Day Time Thoughts

Today's prayer:

_____

_____

_____

_____

Bible Verse(s) I will meditate on today:

_____

_____

_____

_____

Today, I affirm:

_____

_____

_____

_____

Day 2: _____

Nighttime Thoughts

Today, I stepped out in faith by:

_____
_____
_____
_____

And it made me feel:

_____
_____
_____

I spent time with God by:

_____
_____
_____
_____

Day 3: _____

Day Time Thoughts

Today's prayer:

_____

_____

_____

_____

Bible Verse(s) I will meditate on today:

_____

_____

_____

_____

I'm trusting God to:

_____

_____

_____

_____

Day 3: _____

Nighttime Thoughts

Today, I obeyed God by:

_____

_____

_____

_____

Today, I started/stopped:

_____

_____

_____

_____

Today, I was honest with God about:

_____

_____

_____

_____

_____

Day 4: _____

Day Time Thoughts

Today's prayer:

_____
_____
_____
_____

Bible Verse(s) I will meditate on today:

_____
_____
_____
_____

Today, I speak over:

_____
_____
_____
_____
_____

Day 4: _____

Nighttime Thoughts

I would describe today as:

_____
_____
_____
_____

I'm making it easier for God to direct me by:

_____
_____
_____
_____

Today, I forgave/started working on forgiving:

_____
_____
_____
_____

Day 5: _____

Day Time Thoughts

Today's prayer:

_____

_____

_____

_____

Bible Verse(s) I will meditate on today:

_____

_____

_____

_____

Today, I believe:

_____

_____

_____

_____

_____

Day 5: _____

Nighttime Thoughts

Today, I learned:

_____

_____

_____

_____

Based on today, I will start to work on:

_____

_____

_____

_____

Today, I see growth:

_____

_____

_____

_____

_____

Day 6: _____

Day Time Thoughts

Today's prayer:

_____
_____
_____
_____

Bible Verse(s) I will meditate on today:

_____
_____
_____
_____

Today, I declare:

_____
_____
_____
_____

Day 6: _____

Nighttime Thoughts

I showed love today by:

_____

_____

_____

_____

Today, I followed God by:

_____

_____

_____

_____

Today, I became aware of:

_____

_____

_____

_____

_____

Day 7: _____

Day Time Thoughts

Today's prayer:

_____

_____

_____

_____

Bible Verse(s) I will meditate on today:

_____

_____

_____

_____

Today, I trust God for:

_____

_____

_____

_____

Day 7: _____

Nighttime Thoughts

Today, I resisted the enemy by:

_____
_____
_____
_____

I felt God's presence today when:

_____
_____
_____
_____

I want to begin:

_____
_____
_____
_____

Self-Reflection

Week 5 Spiritual Progress

She Prays...

...and mountains

move!

Spiritual Goals for This Week

Prayer Plan For This Week

WEDNESDAY

MY PRAYER TIME:

OBSTACLES THAT MAY PREVENT ME FROM PRAYING THAT DAY.

HOW WILL I AVOID OR OVERCOME?

TUESDAY

MY PRAYER TIME:

OBSTACLES THAT MAY PREVENT ME FROM PRAYING THAT DAY.

HOW WILL I AVOID OR OVERCOME?

MONDAY

MY PRAYER TIME:

OBSTACLES THAT MAY PREVENT ME FROM PRAYING THAT DAY.

HOW WILL I AVOID OR OVERCOME?

Prayer Plan For This Week

THURSDAY

MY PRAYER TIME:

OBSTACLES THAT MAY PREVENT ME FROM PRAYING THAT DAY.

HOW WILL I AVOID OR OVERCOME?

FRIDAY

MY PRAYER TIME:

OBSTACLES THAT MAY PREVENT ME FROM PRAYING THAT DAY.

HOW WILL I AVOID OR OVERCOME?

SATURDAY

MY PRAYER TIME:

OBSTACLES THAT MAY PREVENT ME FROM PRAYING THAT DAY.

HOW WILL I AVOID OR OVERCOME?

Prayer Plan For This Week

NOTES

SUNDAY

MY PRAYER TIME:

OBSTACLES THAT MAY PREVENT ME FROM PRAYING THAT DAY.

HOW WILL I AVOID OR OVERCOME?

Prayer Wall

She Prays | Just Be You Movement | Page 146

God's Timing

Week 6 Devotional

"But Abram said, "Sovereign Lord, what can you give me since I remain childless and the one who will inherit my estate is Eliezer of Damascus?" And Abram said, "You have given me no children; so a servant in my household will be my heir." Then the word of the Lord came to him: "This man will not be your heir, but a son who is your own flesh and blood will be your heir." He took him outside and said, "Look up at the sky and count the stars—if indeed you can count them." Then he said to him, "So shall your offspring[b] be." Abram believed the Lord, and he credited it to him as righteousness."
(Genesis 15:2-6 NIV).

Have you ever had a relationship with someone in a different time zone? It would be a part of your routine to check the time before you call to know whether or not you will get through. Though God is available 24/7 to hear us and bless us, sometimes, due to the time difference between God and us, we must wait.

God promises to make everything beautiful in His time. From where God stands, He is not limited to seeing only the present, but He's omniscient. Therefore, He knows what the future holds. He knows what you need and when would be the best time to give it to you. Sometimes, we must wait, and as difficult and painful as it is, it has a purpose. The waiting process is intended to build your strength and ability to endure (See Isaiah 40:31).

In the above passage, we see how Abraham was in a tight spot. Abraham saw others have children, and he had not yet had one. Witnessing others receiving the very blessings you have been praying for and waiting on is not easy. While you watch them receive favor right before your eyes, the devil jumps at the opportunity to state the obvious and to force an impulsive reaction out of you. For example, he tells you:

"You are getting old, and you have no husband yet," so you get anxious.

"You have been out of a job for two years, and your bills are months past due," so you get impatient.

"You have tried to have children for five years," so you get upset and distance yourself from God.

The enemy wants you to get emotional about your situation so you may react and truly get in the way of your blessing.

*"Against all hope, Abraham in hope **believed** and so became the father of many nations, just as it had been said to him, "So shall your offspring be." (Romans 4:18 – NIV).*

Do not allow the devil to rob you of your hope in Christ. It is okay to get frustrated and sad, but when these emotions come, find yourself seeking God's face. He will replace your human feelings with spiritual conviction. He will continue to give you something to hold on to. He understands your position and your frustration. He factored in your impatience about this entire situation, and He is telling you today to *"be still and know that I'm God."* (See Psalm 46:10). *"It is I who made you, and you are His..."* (See Psalm 100:3).

To be still means to be at peace and when you feel your peace is being haunted by the worst scenario, go to God again and again. Yell and scream, cry and get upset, but do it before God. He will replace your sadness with joy. He will replace your anger with the peace that passeth all understanding.

Day 1: _____

Day Time Thoughts

Today's prayer:

_____
_____
_____
_____

Bible Verse(s) I will meditate on today:

_____
_____
_____
_____

Today, I will work on:

_____
_____
_____
_____

Day 1: _____

Nighttime Thoughts

Today, God showed me:

_____

_____

_____

_____

What I did differently today that helped me feel closer to God:

_____

_____

_____

_____

I helped someone today by:

_____

_____

_____

_____

Day 2: _____

Day Time Thoughts

Today's prayer:

_____
_____
_____
_____

Bible Verse(s) I will meditate on today:

_____
_____
_____
_____

Today, I affirm:

_____
_____
_____
_____
_____

Day 2: _____

Nighttime Thoughts

Today, I stepped out in faith by:

_____
_____
_____
_____

And it made me feel:

_____
_____
_____

I spent time with God by:

_____
_____
_____
_____

Day 3: _____

Day Time Thoughts

Today's prayer:

_____
_____
_____
_____

Bible Verse(s) I will meditate on today:

_____
_____
_____
_____

I'm trusting God to:

_____
_____
_____
_____

Day 3: _____

Nighttime Thoughts

Today, I obeyed God by:

_____

_____

_____

_____

Today, I started/stopped:

_____

_____

_____

_____

Today, I was honest with God about:

_____

_____

_____

_____

_____

_____

Day 4: _____

Day Time Thoughts

Today's prayer:

_____
_____
_____
_____

Bible Verse(s) I will meditate on today:

_____
_____
_____
_____

Today, I speak over:

_____
_____
_____
_____

Day 4: _____

Nighttime Thoughts

I would describe today as:

_____

_____

_____

_____

I'm making it easier for God to direct me by:

_____

_____

_____

_____

Today, I forgave/started working on forgiving:

_____

_____

_____

_____

_____

Day 5: _____

Day Time Thoughts

Today's prayer:

_____

_____

_____

_____

Bible Verse(s) I will meditate on today:

_____

_____

_____

_____

Today, I believe:

_____

_____

_____

_____

_____

Day 5: _____

Nighttime Thoughts

Today, I learned:

_____
_____
_____
_____

Based on today, I will start to work on:

_____
_____
_____
_____

Today, I see growth:

_____
_____
_____
_____

Day 6: _____

Day Time Thoughts

Today's prayer:

_____

_____

_____

_____

Bible Verse(s) I will meditate on today:

_____

_____

_____

_____

Today, I declare:

_____

_____

_____

_____

_____

Day 6: _____

Nighttime Thoughts

I showed love today by:

_____
_____
_____
_____

Today, I followed God by:

_____
_____
_____
_____

Today, I became aware of:

_____
_____
_____
_____
_____

Day 7: _____

Day Time Thoughts

Today's prayer:

_____
_____
_____
_____

Bible Verse(s) I will meditate on today:

_____
_____
_____
_____

Today, I trust God for:

_____
_____
_____
_____

Day 7: _____

Nighttime Thoughts

Today, I resisted the enemy by:

_____

_____

_____

_____

I felt God's presence today when:

_____

_____

_____

_____

I want to begin:

_____

_____

_____

_____

Self-Reflection

Week 6 Spiritual Progress

_____

_____

_____

_____

_____

_____

_____

_____

_____

_____

_____

_____

_____

_____

She Prays...

...and the angels assemble at her request.

Spiritual Goals for This Week

Prayer Plan For This Week

MONDAY

MY PRAYER TIME:

OBSTACLES THAT MAY PREVENT ME FROM PRAYING THAT DAY.

HOW WILL I AVOID OR OVERCOME?

TUESDAY

MY PRAYER TIME:

OBSTACLES THAT MAY PREVENT ME FROM PRAYING THAT DAY.

HOW WILL I AVOID OR OVERCOME?

WEDNESDAY

MY PRAYER TIME:

OBSTACLES THAT MAY PREVENT ME FROM PRAYING THAT DAY.

HOW WILL I AVOID OR OVERCOME?

Prayer Plan For This Week

THURSDAY

MY PRAYER TIME:

OBSTACLES THAT MAY PREVENT ME FROM PRAYING THAT DAY.

HOW WILL I AVOID OR OVERCOME?

FRIDAY

MY PRAYER TIME:

OBSTACLES THAT MAY PREVENT ME FROM PRAYING THAT DAY.

HOW WILL I AVOID OR OVERCOME?

SATURDAY

MY PRAYER TIME:

OBSTACLES THAT MAY PREVENT ME FROM PRAYING THAT DAY.

HOW WILL I AVOID OR OVERCOME?

Prayer Plan For This Week

NOTES

SUNDAY

MY PRAYER TIME:

OBSTACLES THAT MAY PREVENT ME FROM PRAYING THAT DAY.

HOW WILL I AVOID OR OVERCOME?

Prayer Wall

You Belong To Him!

Week 7 Devotional

"For our struggle is not against flesh and blood, but against the rulers, against the authorities, against the powers of this dark world and against the spiritual forces of evil in the heavenly realms." (Ephesians 6:12 – NIV).

It is imperative that as a believer, we remember that we belong to God. Being in this world, and filled with the influence of the world, we often forget that "We wrestle not against flesh and blood." (See Ephesians 6:12). We often find ourselves reacting to things with our flesh and emotions. We need to pay attention to the root of all things that we face. Ask yourself, "Where is this coming from?" We must remember God's warning to us through Paul's writing.

God warns us that if we are led by our flesh in dealing with the enemy, or in dealing with tests of life, we will fail miserably. As women who belong to Christ, and are of the Spirit, we need to look at everything first from a spiritual perspective and be led by the Holy Spirit.

If you are employed by a company, you deal with situations according to the company's policies.

When in a marriage, you and your spouse agree to the best way to handle situations that is conducive to the betterment of your relationship. Likewise, when you are in Christ, you are to deal with things in a way that is best for your relationship with Christ, and in a way that properly represents your union with Him. Hence, you cannot first address attacks, problems, difficulties, or any situations in the flesh.

The bible asks us as humans who are limited in our understanding of the things of the spirit, to seek first the kingdom of God and all other things (including solutions and answers to your issues) will be given to you. We belong to God, and He will reveal all truths to us once we seek Him

Day 1: _____

Day Time Thoughts

Today's prayer:

_____

_____

_____

_____

Bible Verse(s) I will meditate on today:

_____

_____

_____

_____

Today, I will work on:

_____

_____

_____

_____

_____

Day 1: _____

Nighttime Thoughts

Today, God showed me:

_____
_____
_____
_____

What I did differently today that helped me feel closer to God:

_____
_____
_____
_____

I helped someone today by:

_____
_____
_____
_____

Day 2: _____

Day Time Thoughts

Today's prayer:

_____
_____
_____
_____

Bible Verse(s) I will meditate on today:

_____
_____
_____
_____

Today, I affirm:

_____
_____
_____
_____
_____

Day 2: _____

Nighttime Thoughts

Today, I stepped out in faith by:

_____

_____

_____

_____

And it made me feel:

_____

_____

_____

I spent time with God by:

_____

_____

_____

_____

Day 3: _____

Day Time Thoughts

Today's prayer:

_____

_____

_____

_____

Bible Verse(s) I will meditate on today:

_____

_____

_____

I'm trusting God to:

_____

_____

_____

_____

_____

Day 3: _____

Nighttime Thoughts

Today, I obeyed God by:

_____

_____

_____

_____

Today, I started/stopped:

_____

_____

_____

_____

Today, I was honest with God about:

_____

_____

_____

_____

_____

Day 4: _____

Day Time Thoughts

Today's prayer:

_____
_____
_____
_____

Bible Verse(s) I will meditate on today:

_____
_____
_____

Today, I speak over:

_____
_____
_____
_____

Day 4: _____

Nighttime Thoughts

I would describe today as:

_____
_____
_____
_____

I'm making it easier for God to direct me by:

_____
_____
_____
_____

Today, I forgave/started working on forgiving:

_____
_____
_____
_____

Day 5: _____

Day Time Thoughts

Today's prayer:

_____

_____

_____

_____

Bible Verse(s) I will meditate on today:

_____

_____

_____

Today, I believe:

_____

_____

_____

_____

Day 5: _____

Nighttime Thoughts

Today, I learned:

_____
_____
_____
_____

Based on today, I will start to work on:

_____
_____
_____
_____

Today, I see growth:

_____
_____
_____
_____

Day 6: _____

Day Time Thoughts

Today's prayer:

_____

_____

_____

_____

Bible Verse(s) I will meditate on today:

_____

_____

_____

_____

Today, I declare:

_____

_____

_____

_____

_____

Day 6: _____

Nighttime Thoughts

I showed love today by:

_____
_____
_____
_____

Today, I followed God by:

_____
_____
_____
_____

Today, I became aware of:

_____
_____
_____
_____

Day 7: _____

Day Time Thoughts

Today's prayer:

_____

_____

_____

_____

Bible Verse(s) I will meditate on today:

_____

_____

_____

Today, I trust God for:

_____

_____

_____

_____

_____

Day 7: _____

Nighttime Thoughts

Today, I resisted the enemy by:

_____
_____
_____
_____

I felt God's presence today when:

_____
_____
_____
_____

I want to begin:

_____
_____
_____
_____
_____

Self-Reflection

Week 7 Spiritual Progress

She Prays...

...knowing life and death are in the power of her words.

Spiritual Goals for This Week

Prayer Plan For This Week

MONDAY

MY PRAYER TIME:

OBSTACLES THAT MAY PREVENT ME FROM PRAYING THAT DAY.

HOW WILL I AVOID OR OVERCOME?

TUESDAY

MY PRAYER TIME:

OBSTACLES THAT MAY PREVENT ME FROM PRAYING THAT DAY.

HOW WILL I AVOID OR OVERCOME?

WEDNESDAY

MY PRAYER TIME:

OBSTACLES THAT MAY PREVENT ME FROM PRAYING THAT DAY.

HOW WILL I AVOID OR OVERCOME?

Prayer Plan For This Week

THURSDAY

MY PRAYER TIME:

OBSTACLES THAT MAY PREVENT ME FROM PRAYING THAT DAY.

HOW WILL I AVOID OR OVERCOME?

FRIDAY

MY PRAYER TIME:

OBSTACLES THAT MAY PREVENT ME FROM PRAYING THAT DAY.

HOW WILL I AVOID OR OVERCOME?

SATURDAY

MY PRAYER TIME:

OBSTACLES THAT MAY PREVENT ME FROM PRAYING THAT DAY.

HOW WILL I AVOID OR OVERCOME?

Prayer Plan For This Week

NOTES

SUNDAY

MY PRAYER TIME:

OBSTACLES THAT MAY PREVENT ME FROM PRAYING THAT DAY.

HOW WILL I AVOID OR OVERCOME?

Prayer Wall

You Have All That You Need

Week 8 Devotional

"For if you possess these qualities in increasing measure, they will keep you from being ineffective and unproductive in your knowledge of our Lord Jesus Christ." (2 Peter 1:3-8 – NIV).

The moment you accept Jesus into your heart, you have answered the call on your life, as no man can come to the Father unless the Spirit of God draws him. You then receive the Holy Spirit along with the fruits of the Spirit. The fruit of the Spirit helps you to grow in God, but it is important to note that only what you feed will grow.

But the fruit of the Spirit is love, joy, peace, forbearance, kindness, goodness, faithfulness, gentleness, and self-control (Galatians 5:22-23a – NIV).

Peter encourages us to note that it is not enough just to have one characteristic but to add on to it so that we become more effective. According to 2 Peter 1:3-7:

YOU HAVE:	ADD ON
FAITH	GOODNESS
GOODNESS	KNOWLEDGE
KNOWLEDGE	SELF-CONTROL
SELF-CONTROL	PERSEVERANCE
PERSEVERANCE	GODLINESS
GODLINESS	MUTUAL AFFECTION
MUTUAL AFFECTION	LOVE

There is always more to be done and room for growth. There is room to excel further by identifying, correcting, and learning. The addition of the knowledge of God is not only for the pastors or church leaders, but we all must explain our beliefs. It is not enough to only have faith in God, but also to have self-control, to know our limits and not be triggered by everything. Living a life that is pleasing to God requires us to possess a range of characteristics and requires us to work, build, and grow.

The aim is not to attain perfection but to always aim to make more progress. We cannot become complacent at any phase of our Christian walk. It is not enough to only recognize your strengths but to know and work on your weaknesses. The enemy will come after your weaknesses and will tempt you according to your desires.

"When tempted, no one should say, "God is tempting me." For God cannot be tempted by evil, nor does he tempt anyone; but each person is tempted when they are dragged away by their own evil desire and enticed. Then, after desire has conceived, it gives birth to sin; and sin, when it is full-grown, gives birth to death" (James 1:13-15 - NIV).

If we possess these qualities listed in the table (according to 2 Peter 1:3-7) increasingly, it will keep us from being ineffective and unproductive. It will keep us from easily falling short of the glory of God. We will be kept from growing weary in this faith walk and from doubting God when He doesn't give us what we want, in the timing that we want it.

As you wait on God to bring your husband, to give you a child, to give you your dream job, to give you a bigger house, to expand your company or to give you an idea for a new business, don't sit there idly doing nothing. There is a lot of work to be done and a lot of growing to do. Go water your fruits in the word of God and do what is needed for them to blossom into trees. This is so you may have an entire field of faith and not just a mustard seed. God wants you to have acres of love and joy, enough to go around. You have what you need to survive and thrive.

Day 1: _____

Day Time Thoughts

Today's prayer:

_____
_____
_____
_____

Bible Verse(s) I will meditate on today:

_____
_____
_____
_____

Today, I will work on:

_____
_____
_____
_____
_____

Day 1: _____

Nighttime Thoughts

Today, God showed me:

_____
_____
_____
_____

What I did differently today that helped me feel closer to God:

_____
_____
_____
_____

I helped someone today by:

_____
_____
_____
_____

Day 2: _____

Day Time Thoughts

Today's prayer:

_____

_____

_____

_____

Bible Verse(s) I will meditate on today:

_____

_____

_____

_____

Today, I affirm:

_____

_____

_____

_____

Day 2: _____

Nighttime Thoughts

Today, I stepped out in faith by:

_____

_____

_____

_____

And it made me feel:

_____

_____

_____

I spent time with God by:

_____

_____

_____

_____

Day 3: _____

Day Time Thoughts

Today's prayer:

_____

_____

_____

_____

Bible Verse(s) I will meditate on today:

_____

_____

_____

_____

I'm trusting God to:

_____

_____

_____

_____

_____

Day 3: _____

Nighttime Thoughts

Today, I obeyed God by:

_____

_____

_____

_____

Today, I started/stopped:

_____

_____

_____

_____

Today, I was honest with God about:

_____

_____

_____

_____

_____

Day 4: _____

Day Time Thoughts

Today's prayer:

_____

_____

_____

_____

Bible Verse(s) I will meditate on today:

_____

_____

_____

_____

Today, I speak over:

_____

_____

_____

_____

Day 4: _____

Nighttime Thoughts

I would describe today as:

_____
_____
_____
_____

I'm making it easier for God to direct me by:

_____
_____
_____

Today, I forgave/started working on forgiving:

_____
_____
_____
_____
_____

Day 5: _____

Day Time Thoughts

Today's prayer:

_____

_____

_____

_____

Bible Verse(s) I will meditate on today:

_____

_____

_____

_____

Today, I believe:

_____

_____

_____

_____

_____

Day 5: _____

Nighttime Thoughts

Today, I learned:

_____
_____
_____
_____

Based on today, I will start to work on:

_____
_____
_____
_____

Today, I see growth:

_____
_____
_____
_____

Day 6: _____

Day Time Thoughts

Today's prayer:

_____

_____

_____

_____

Bible Verse(s) I will meditate on today:

_____

_____

_____

_____

Today, I declare:

_____

_____

_____

_____

Day 6: _____

Nighttime Thoughts

I showed love today by:

_____

_____

_____

_____

Today, I followed God by:

_____

_____

_____

_____

Today, I became aware of:

_____

_____

_____

_____

_____

Day 7: _____

Day Time Thoughts

Today's prayer:

_____
_____
_____
_____

Bible Verse(s) I will meditate on today:

_____
_____
_____
_____

Today, I trust God for:

_____
_____
_____
_____
_____

Day 7: _____

Nighttime Thoughts

Today, I resisted the enemy by:

_____
_____
_____
_____

I felt God's presence today when:

_____
_____
_____

I want to begin:

_____
_____
_____
_____

Self-Reflection

Week 8 Spiritual Progress

_____
_____
_____
_____
_____
_____
_____
_____
_____
_____
_____
_____
_____

She Prays...

...and she

will not fail!